N. Anagnos

Walk These Stones

Encounters along a Costa Rican village road

Leslie Hawthorne Klingler

Paintings by Dotty Hawthorne

*To Lyell and Johnnie,
Enjoy the "Walk"
Dotty Hawthorne*

SQUIRE OAKS PRESS
SAN LUIS OBISPO, CALIFORNIA

Walk These Stones

Encounters along a Costa Rican village road

Published by Squire Oaks Press, San Luis Obispo, California
squireoakspress@aol.com

Scripture quotations are taken from the *Holy Bible,* New Living Translation,
Copyright ©1996. Used by permission of Tyndale House Publishers, Inc.,
Wheaton, Illinois 60189. All rights reserved.

Graphic design by Ashala Lawler

Printing and binding by Jostens, Visalia, California

ISBN: 0-9712664-0-9

DEDICATION
To the people of Cuatro Cruces

THANKS TO

Shelley, for inviting me to follow in your footsteps as you dance salsa

Jim and Gary, for ink to write about the courage you have given me

Dotty, for the color of creativity with love

Susan, for teaching me to sing the stones

Nita, Betty, Bill

and my best friend, Tim

Contents

STONES

Look at these stones with me. Wipe the tropical sweat off your brow and kneel here in the road in front of my home. Look at these stones, all shapes and sizes: tiny pebbles like the one stuck in your shoe; smooth, flat stones perfect for puddle skipping; and the big, chalky rock fringed with persistent green.

Kneel with me before this swath of stone strewn like the stars of the universe, stretching from the highway, through the village, and far into the mountains beyond my home.

These pieces of planet are wet and silver as the afternoon sky, pushed into the slick, red mud by bicycles, oxcarts, and an occasional motorcycle or car, polished with the tread of rubber boots, sandals, and Sunday shoes.

Look at these stones with me. They tell stories, these stones that mold into the arch of feet, stub toes, harden muscles, and determine the way I will go.

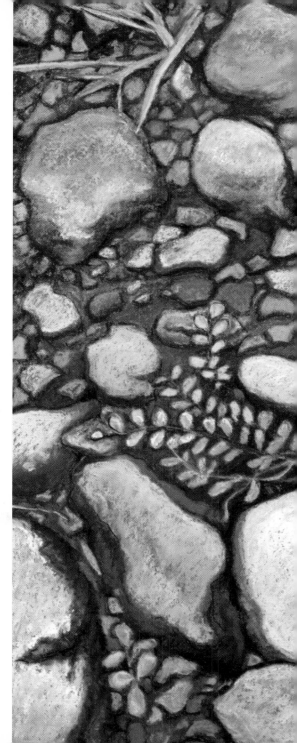

Stones on a village road

María and Goyo's home

A NEW DAY

I awake in a thick blanket of warm air. The backs of my eyelids glow stained-glass red from sunlight pouring through cracks in the walls. The walls are porous to light and to sounds of my host family beginning a new day. I hear the woman urging her eight-year-old boy and twelve-year-old girl to dress for school. I barely know her yet; her name is María.

I watch the sheet rise and fall with my breathing, then stretch and touch my husband's face. We are bare; we bring nothing to this place but our smiles, our laughter, and the strange words that stumble off our tongues. We offer no complicated words, no sophisticated skills. I feel like a child dressed in the warmth of summertime.

Everything is new and it alerts my senses. I emerge from the mosquito net and my feet feel the smooth, freshly waxed floorboards. I dress, noticing my skin's texture and the weave of my clothes, then listen to my flip-flops slap a path toward the outhouse. I hear the sagging porch gate squeak "be gentle" as I open it and chickens cluck insistently for their morning grain.

We eat breakfast with the boy and girl at a small wooden table on the old porch. Smartly dressed in white and navy uniforms, the children rock the table with their elbows as they scoop fried rice and black beans with spoons too big for their mouths. Eyes black and round, they watch us from behind the speckled mounds on their spoons.

María calls from the kitchen, warning the children they will be late for school. The two wipe their mouths with the back of their hands and scramble off, leaving the blue tablecloth littered with small islands of rice and beans.

We continue eating in silence, smoke seeping through the wall that divides the porch from the kitchen's wood-burning stove. The smoke tastes like wispy curls of onion, and the onions in our rice and beans smell of smoke.

María clears our plates and smiles shyly when we thank her. As we stand to leave, she tells us lunch will be ready at noon.

The stony road is still damp from last night's rain. It ushers us through green fields dotted with tropical laurels, straight and naked as totem poles, and mango trees laden with hundreds of tiny, embryo-shaped fruit. A flock of parakeets flies overhead singing a rowdy morningsong and long-eared Brahma cattle raise their heads to observe us as we pass by. In the distance, indigo hills contemplate us, reverent before three volcanoes etched in a cobalt sky.

As we walk along the road, I feel washed clean by the rains of change. The pain of leaving home recedes as I enter this place – new and rich in its apparent simplicity. I am rich too, because my feet curve with the stones in the road, because the sun shines golden, and because my friend and I travel lightly, holding hands.

ON FARMING AND THE KINGDOM

*E*arly-morning sunshine draws last night's rain from the damp earth, moistening the air. My rubber boots chafe at the anklebone as I walk along the uneven road.

I carry a new *macana*. María's husband, Goyo, cut down two small saplings, stripped their bark, then fitted the new poles with flat, metal blades like giant chisels. He handed the new tools to my husband and me and told us we were ready to farm.

Tim and I pass a dozen homes, waving to women hanging laundry on barbed-wire fences, uniformed children walking to school, and men riding bicycles to their fields. On the village outskirts, we slosh across a shallow stream and enter Don Dimas' property.

Juan and José Benito, brothers by faith and friendship, are already in the field helping their neighbor plant his corn. Don Dimas is too weak to plant his three acres alone, and two of his sons have moved away to work at factories in the capital. The third works at a heart-of-palm processing plant in a nearby town and says the work and wages of a farmer are cruel. Seeing their neighbor's need, Juan and José Benito step in to help like the sons many local farmers wish they had.

We stand under a low tree and watch the three men planting along long rows marked off with twine. Using *macanas*, they pierce the dark earth, lifting the soil while simultaneously reaching for seed in containers tied around their waists. They deftly fling three kernels into the holes, then remove their *macanas* so dirt covers the seeds as they step one pace forward, stabbing the soil again. The trio moves in quick rhythm, piercing the earth and throwing the seed.

Several minutes later, the men stop planting and join us under the tree. Gulping water from old bleach bottles, they invite us to work with them.

Tim teams up with José Benito, who is small and lithe and plants with graceful ease. José Benito is quiet, soft-spoken, and still slightly timid with us, though Tim's jokes make him break into a cherubic grin. José Benito owns no land but has farmed borrowed plots for more than a decade. Since he was ten years old, his small earnings have helped sustain his mother and five siblings.

I overhear José Benito and Tim converse as they plant, long spaces filling their dialogue in the leisure of ample time. Prompted by Tim's curiosity and frequent inquiries, José Benito explains a typical cycle of planting and selling their two major crops: corn and beans. Tim adds expenses then subtracts them from potential earnings. The result surprises me; the amount seems insufficient for a family's subsistence. And I remember Don Dimas' son describing last year's drought and the previous year's floods – two agricultural cycles with almost no harvest. I wonder how the family survives.

Several rows away, I work alongside Juan, whose red baseball cap plasters his jet-black bangs to his forehead. I sense his presence differently since our walk together last Saturday afternoon, when he disclosed a glimpse of his past to Tim and me. I do not know how the unusual opportunity came up – this detailed admission into a *campesino's* personal history. Juan shared about his life during the Nicaraguan civil war, recalling memories as if he were pulling tarnished medals from a forgotten closet, polishing them, and rediscovering their gleam. A thirteen-year-old drafted into the Sandinista army, he defected with a group of even younger boys. He described how he and his

> **I think of the many villagers I have met in the past months; each face is only as simple as the depth of my acquaintance.**

comrades stole through the jungle with the intuition of frightened prey, fleeing the Sandinistas as defectors and the Contras as enemies. They evaded land mines, swam across the San Juan River, then exchanged guns for decent treatment with the Costa Rican border patrol. After two years in a refugee camp, Juan found his way to Cuatro Cruces.

Wiping my forehead with the back of my hand powdered with the insecticide that coats the seeds, I contemplate the logic of my new respect for Juan. I think of the many villagers I have met in the past months; each face is only as simple as the depth of my acquaintance.

Don Dimas plants alone a short distance from the four of us. His face, shadowed by a worn cotton hat, communicates little more than sun-weathered years. Juan tells me that Don Dimas, one of the village's first settlers, carved

these fields from thick, virgin jungle. Don Dimas is one of the village majority who are Catholic yet maintain a good relationship with the *evangélicos* of the local Mennonite church.

I wonder if Don Dimas thinks we get in the way, until I notice him discreetly observing us and responding to our clumsy efforts to plant with a kind smile. Unfamiliarity's barrier broken, we soon converse easily. He tells about the good old days of predictable weather patterns and generous soil.

By mid-morning, my clothes are soaked through and stick like cellophane to my chest and thighs. I lean on my *macana*. Juan already works far ahead of me and I am exhausted by my awkward attempts to farm. My eyes trace the deep furrows, the color of burnt umber, carved into a wealthier neighbor's field by an oxen-drawn plow, then

I look up at the blue sky embroidered with distant clouds. I can almost hear music (it is strange and wonderful), a sweaty song of sunshine yet rumbling of storms and rain.

I observe Juan, José Benito, and Don Dimas as they work, burnished muscles dancing in their arms. They are lean and sweating and unaware that they move with a rhythm that sustains the centuries, pulsing life through and beyond the grandeur of civilizations and their kings. History books record royalty and ruins, but like these men, history's multitudes have shaped their lives around earth and seed and open fields.

They will have good company in heaven, I imagine. Generations of farmers from every nation will sustain the new creation's song. Delighting in rich soil and soft rains, they will reap together unrivaled harvests.

I step forward again, my palm already blistered from the *macana* and the back of my neck burning in the sun. Juan waves as he comes back toward me, planting another row. Perhaps this experience will allow me to fully appreciate the new earth's fertility. Perhaps these men will teach me to reap a greater harvest of heaven's joy.

José Benito

HARVEST HOME

After three months of muggy heat and constant rain, tall corn urges villagers to harvest. I swing gently in a hammock in our living room, fingering a silver chain around my neck and listening to afternoon rain dance on the tin roof. I savor the fruit of kindness: this new home.

Two months ago, José Benito, the coordinator of the church leadership team, offered the abandoned parsonage to us rent-free. Concluding a tour, he informed us, "We decided you can live here for three years – or as long as you want. After all, you might decide to stay forever." José Benito smiles like an angel. The dusty rooms exuded potential home, so Tim and I said we would like to fix it up and rent it.

New friends found us a home and our home found us new friends. When we arrived for our first day of house repairs, we encountered the place bustling with church members. Nineteen-year-old Víctor poured the cement porch with

Goyo, Don Dimas' son-in-law. The two sang enthusiastically as they worked:

There is a fiesta, fiesta, fiesta,
a never-ending fiesta inside of me!

There is a fiesta, fiesta, fiesta,
since I met Jesus!

Inside, twenty-year-old Saida swept the rafters. She welcomed us with silver cob-webs in her coal-black hair. Juan, wearing his red baseball cap, chased bats out of the bedroom with a broom. He stopped to shake our hands only after the bats had swooped by us, circled the room, then reluctantly escaped out the back door. José Benito's little brother, Anival, wearing a broken pair of sunglasses he found while exploring the house, plowed through us making motorcycle noises. Seventy-year-old Benilda called to us from the bedroom, kneeling on the cement floor and proudly displaying a scorpion flattened on the sole of her flip-flop. (José Benito, alerting us to Benilda's feistiness, told us she decided to build her own house last year. After discovering her intentions when she asked to borrow a saw, he convened men from the church to assist her.)

José Benito worked far more than other church members, arriving early and staying late for almost a month. Using a hammer, handsaw, and machete, he resourcefully straightened bent nails, patched holes in tin, and pieced together scrap wood – salvaging all he could.

We soon discovered the challenge of transporting building materials to Cuatro Cruces and marveled at José Benito's ability to balance long two-by-fours and hundred-pound bags of cement on his bicycle. I first heard José Benito and Tim laughing like friends while the villager taught the *gringo* how to do the same.

Maintaining a constant stream of candid dialogue, Saida and I began to weave our worlds together as we painted the house and prepared lunch for the workers. One of the few local women with a high school diploma, Saida left the village in search of employment soon after her graduation. She worked in a factory in the capital for two years, then returned home as a new Christian, convinced that God wanted her to care for her ailing mother and support the village church.

During the course of our days together, I noticed Saida stop her work periodically, listening for José Benito's laughter and footsteps. Whenever he approached, however, she appeared too focused on painting or cooking to even glance up at the young man.

Breeze blows on me through the open window. I smile at the memory of those first days of new friendship. These clean, red-waxed floors and new wood walls glow with the work of dozens of hands.

I look down at the small pendant on the chain around my neck; it says "Ruth," my grandmother's name, in rounded, flowing cursive. I think about my neighbors harvesting their corn and con-sider my middle name. Like the Moabite whose name my grandmother and I share, I harvest kindness in a new land.

HOMESICKNESS

*C*hristmas falls during a soggy week in the final hurrah of the rainy season. A steady shower on the tin roof has drowned the silence for hours, and even the porous ground outside our home squishes under my feet. The impatiens lining our porch stretch their bright, happy faces while the roses droop and tomato plants wilt. I must be a rose or a tomato.

My lethargy began when outsiders invaded Cuatro Cruces two days before Christmas. I intended to visit Don Dimas, but nearing his house, I saw that it was filled with unfamiliar faces. My clothes damp with drizzle, I paused to observe the newcomers – most likely Don Dimas' grown children and their families visiting for the week-long break from factory jobs in the city. Lacking the energy to converse with strangers, I turned around and headed back the way I had come. I ached for a home where I knew I belonged.

Every Christmas week, dozens of relatives arrive from out of town and spend entire days relaxing together in crowded village homes. Activities center around tamale preparation, which includes killing the Christmas pig (invariably nicknamed *Navidad*), and watching television programs depicting snow and sleigh bells and boxes with bows.

The Cuatro Cruces church pays little attention to the religious significance of Christmas. I am uncertain whether the reason for this is the absence of tradition or the fact that church members dismiss the religious calendar when they abandon Catholicism. Holy days seem to imply rituals associated with what they define as their "old man": before they had a life-changing encounter with Jesus. Even normal midweek services are suspended during the holidays, so our little church remains closed and silent.

Christmas Eve feels too quiet and ordinary. I work in the garden, acutely aware of being thousands of miles from Christmas carols, stockings, presents, and cranberries. (I have yet to find the Spanish translation for cranberries.) By evening, my mood is as gloomy as the gray sky. I rinse my work clothes in a bucket and the water churns deep terracotta. The house feels dirty and damp.

Tim enters the back door with mud-stained clothes and wet hair standing on end. He washes a prize garden squash then proudly shows it to me. Perfectly round and mottled green, it would be a beautiful holiday centerpiece. He slices and boils the squash then blends the meaty orange pulp into a creamy soup.

We eat our simple meal by candlelight. The soup has nutmeg and tastes like pumpkin pie. It begins to warm my insides, which feel cold in seventy-degree temperature – it must be the relentless rain.

We sip the soup. "The day after Christmas is one of the biggest shopping days of the year," I remind him, "and everything will be on sale."

"We can go shopping," Tim jokes. "I'm sure Doña María will have good deals at the storefront in her home: two-for-one potatoes or fifty-percent-off sugar or discount oil – maybe even Jell-O or Kool-Aid."

I groan. Sensing my dour mood, he falls silent, sipping his soup.

I awake at 4 a.m. on Christmas morning. Restless, I get out of bed and wonder what to do with myself. After an unsuccessful attempt to read my Bible, I plug in our old cassette player, scan the bookshelf, and remove a hymnal covered with powdery green mold. Settling on the couch, I select the recording of a church service sent to us last month by our home congregation.

Tim wakes to the four-part harmony and, sleepy-eyed, joins me on the couch. We follow along with the congregation, attempting to sing alto and tenor parts and participating with growing enthusiasm in responsive readings and prayers. The taped voices, struggling against the static of our cassette player, remind me of our community and embrace me in my loneliness.

We sit in silence after the tape clicks off. It is still dark outside. I listen to the unceasing rain and think about cleaning the house, cooking breakfast, feeding the chickens, and perhaps working in the garden. My gladness begins to dawn with the morning. These unremarkable days, uncluttered by holiday tradition, allow me to reflect on Jesus' birth into the ordinary. I imagine Christmas was much like this for women two thousand years ago, tending to their homes and unaware of celestial choirs or unusual events in Bethlehem stables.

Christmas Eve
feels too quiet
and ordinary.
I work in the garden,
acutely aware of being
thousands of miles from
Christmas carols,
stockings, presents,
and cranberries.
By evening, my mood
is as gloomy
as the gray sky.
I rinse my work clothes
in a bucket and the water
churns deep terracotta.
The house feels
dirty and damp.

REVELATION

*J*ulia sits looking out her doorway, the sunset gilding her hair, face, and arms. Her conversation with Nelda, who relaxes in a rocking chair next to her, melts softly like the fading light as I approach and greet them with a blessing: *"Dios les bendiga."*

"Amen," they reply. I say hello to Nelda's twin girls, who smile shyly from a hammock on the porch, dragging their feet to stop its swing. Julia urges me inside and points to a low stool just inside the door. I sit down, casting a long shadow on the wooden walls.

Julia's face, traced with soft lines, is warm and golden. She apologizes for not offering me anything to eat – or even coffee to drink – admitting that all she has in the kitchen is a small bowl of fried rice. I wish I had thought to bring several of the freshly baked muffins sitting on our counter. Julia does not seem to notice my empty hands, however, and she shows obvious delight in my mere presence.

Our conversation ebbs and flows, reaching into subjects such as her health and the possibility of electricity coming to this part of the village, then always returning to reminders of God and his work in our lives. Julia's faith permeates every facet of her world.

The shadows growing, Nelda rises and explains that she wants to walk home before dark. Julia asks when she will visit again. Nelda reminds her that she cannot come on Tuesday or Thursday afternoon because she has class at the local school. "I'm learning to read," she announces to me. "I already understand every letter in the alphabet."

As Nelda calls the twins, Julia confides her plans to take literacy classes next year. The girls yell goodbye from the gate, their slight figures soft in their faded dresses. Julia waves and comments, "I look at those girls and think, 'they don't even realize how blessed they are just to be able to read.'"

She points to a calendar on the wall, its words and images fuzzy in the dim light. "Imagine being able to just look at that and understand it! Or knowing what this says!" She picks up a cup with a phrase in English wrapped around its lip: *"When business interferes with pleasure, give up the business."* I smile and decide not to attempt a translation.

Julia admits she used to blame her family for all her problems. She blamed her father for abandoning her before she was born. She blamed her mother for leaving her when she was eight years old. She blamed the family that

raised her for insisting that all she needed to learn was to cook, clean, plant, and harvest. She confesses that when she became a Christian she had to ask for God's forgiveness for her bitterness towards them for keeping her out of school.

Julia speaks without pause, her soft voice interrupted only when her high cheekbones break into a broad smile. In the background, I hear chickens heading to roost in a nearby tree and the shouts of children returning home from the soccer field.

Julia questions why her literate neighbors read so little. "I'm very observant," she comments. "When I visit people and see their television sitting in the middle of the room like the queen of the house, I wonder, 'Where is their Bible?' I look and look until I spot it stuck in a corner, waiting for the next church service. I ask myself, 'How can they neglect God's Word when they have its secrets open to them?'" She tells me she would read her Bible every day before dawn, after every meal, and before she goes to bed.

Julia explains to me that God shares his Word with her in spite of her illiteracy – that he reveals powerful things when she fasts and gets down on her knees. I think of her curtains glowing with candlelight every time we

Julia

walk by her house at 4:30 a.m. on travel days and am reminded of her morning prayers. Julia, beautiful as the lilies of the field, prays daily for her bread. I do not doubt that God reveals powerful things to her, for her friendship with God radiates from her smile, her laughter, and small things like her sincere thanks for a pineapple. Her life is a constant conversation with her Creator.

Julia assures me that God gets around her not knowing how to read, but imagines there would be nothing better than discovering hidden truths in the Bible. She smiles. "I tell God that I may not be a spring chicken anymore, but as long as I'm living there's hope that someday I'll sit down and read his Word!"

I can no longer see Julia's face in the growing darkness, just her head nodding and hands lifted in harmony with her words. I stand up and tell her I must go. I look forward to seeing her in church.

I step through the doorway, into the night that has already swallowed the sunset, and hurry home following the veiled contour of the road. As my feet tentatively feel their way over the stones, I wonder what it might be like for Julia to read the Bible for the first time. She and her God already converse so easily.

Juan and Ana

CHURCH NEXT DOOR

The church, with peeling paint and a gate that says "*Iglecia Evangélica*" (*Iglesia* misspelled with a "c"), sits just twenty feet from our little house. The rough-hewn benches are packed tight every Sunday with thirty adults and more than fifty children. (The benches used to be roomier, but José Benito sawed off their ends before Ana and Juan's wedding so Ana could proceed down the aisle without snagging her big white dress. Now we sit really close.) About twenty people attend the two midweek services and a dozen women fast and pray here all day Tuesday. A crowd fills the sanctuary and pours out into the entryway during vigils, which last until midnight. In addition, there are Saturday youth services, countless leaders' meetings, guitar practice, and counseling sessions – all just a few paces from our house.

When it comes to attending church, the Cuatro Cruces congregation defies the Latin American concept of time. On Sundays, benches fill more than a half-hour early and only a few people arrive after the formal service begins at 9 a.m. This morning, Saida arrives at 7:30 a.m. to clean the chapel. Tim and I eat breakfast listening to her sing as she sweeps, mops, and straightens benches.

Juan and Ana arrive next, with Juan peddling effortlessly and Ana perched on the crossbar of his gleaming blue bicycle. Juan settles in one of the rocking chairs on our porch and greets us through the open front window. In spite of transporting his short, round wife over hilly terrain, his ironed shirt shows no trace of exertion, and even his unruly black hair is neatly combed. We converse briefly before he heads to the church to tune the old guitar.

Julia and Benilda arrive several minutes later and I hear them begin to pray. Then Auxiliadora, shading herself from the sun with an umbrella, walks up with her son. Anival bangs on our door yelling, "*Hola, Leslie! Tinn!*" He wears his favorite striped shirt and blue jeans that just barely cover his ankles. I crack open the door and inform him we are still getting ready, so he retires to one of the two hammocks on the porch. We hear the *thump-thump* of his feet pushing off the side of our house. Other children soon join him, sitting three to a hammock and thumping against the house.

When we close our windows and latch the door at 8:50 a.m., the church hums with a cheery blend of prayer, conversation, and singing, muted momentarily by the roar of Goyo's motorcycle as he arrives with María and their two children. Goyo's shiny black cowboy boots are the only ones in town. We are greeted by a friendly crowd mingling at the church entryway. José Benito smiles and says he will have to discipline us for arriving late.

José Benito addresses us in playful jest, but his comment makes me wonder how people interpret our arriving only ten minutes before the service. I doubt Cuatro Cruces adheres to traditional Latin American protocol for arriving at gatherings according to one's perception of his or her social rank: insignificant participants arrive the earliest while the most important show up last – making everyone wait but waiting for no one.

Julia told me once that she never arrives late to church because "we need to be on time for God's time."

Contemplating these ideas, I look around at my brothers and sisters; some converse and others sing or kneel at their pews, while children dash around in uninhibited play. I doubt their early arrival to church services has so much to do with social order or even pleasing God as it does with the sheer delight of spending time together.

Her colorful blouse like a bright bouquet behind the lace-covered pulpit, Julia urges those of us outside to come indoors and welcomes us to the service. Holding the microphone so close it buzzes, she invites us to prayer.

LISTEN TO
THE WAVES

Prayer in the Cuatro Cruces church is loud and highly participatory. Individuals simultaneously carry on audible conversations with God: Carmen crying, Jenny shouting, Juan singing, and Alejandra clapping as if making fresh tortillas. The converging voices, intonations, claps and cries rise and fall, ebb and flow. Unless someone becomes exceptionally demonstrative, the prayers blend into the backdrop of my thoughts like the roar of ocean waves.

I first experienced this prayer form as a new service worker eager to embrace my host culture. I remember an evening service in a small church, hot and stuffy with too many bodies and too little air. When the singing evaporated into prayer, the hair on my arms stood on end as spiritual electricity buzzed through me and made my eyes water. My teary prayers rode on the great, rolling waves of the earnest communal intercession.

Five minutes later and my tears dried, I waited for a tidy conclusion from the congregation – a graceful retreat from prayer's holy waters. I waited, eyes closed and head bowed, and waited and waited. Finally, impatience overcame my composure and I looked up. It appeared the people around me failed to notice the heavy accumulation of time. With reverent, earnest expression, voices surging and receding, their prayers went on and on – and that was only the beginning of the service.

Hundreds of church services later, I am learning to pray with my Costa Rican brothers and sisters. But before I could plunge into the new waters, I needed to understand the currents, learn the technique, and recognize my limits to know when to swim to shore.

Understanding these waters meant first reflecting on my own ocean – my own need for prayer. Among other things, it meant realizing I divide my prayer into two very defined and distinct categories: private and public. Private prayers represent my most sincere expressions of myself to God. In contrast, my public prayers are clean, concise, and cautious (or, some may consider, insincere, stilted, and very boring).

The local definition of privacy is far more generous than my own. For example, Jenny mentions enjoying privacy in her home although eight people live in a two-bedroom house. José Benito calls his bicycle his own, yet Víctor and the rest of his family borrow it without asking. Similarly, private prayer has a different meaning to the church here. José Benito kneels at his bench, Víctor turns his face to the wall, Goyo strums the guitar, and Carmen waves her arms; each person converses privately with God, accompanied by the utterances of brothers and sisters around them. Alternatively, during public prayer, each member of the congregation expresses aloud, in his or her own words, an idea or request indicated by the prayer leader. Both public and private prayer are audible and communal and, for the most part, take place in church.

Understanding more about the church's prayer forms, I next needed to learn to ride the waves. Though I might never swim with a native's finesse, I could at least jump in and try. Slowly, I pushed through my inhibitions and comfort zones and began to swim.

And I continue to learn. My reserve no longer holds my hands to my side nor seals my mouth shut. I raise my arms (tentatively) and lift my voice (quietly), and cry if I need to. And when the ebb and flow of prayer drains me and I cease to swim with the swells, I allow myself to walk ashore. I no longer let my own fatigue cause me to judge others' sincerity, nor do I worry about what kind of swimmer they perceive me to be. I simply retreat from the waters, settle on the shore, and open my Bible. It is a good place to read – to the rhythm of the breaking waves.

LOVE SONGS

*W*orship, strung together by a thread of prayer, shines with the beads of singing. Every church service includes singing during times of *adoración* (adoration), *alabanza* (praise), and *especiales* (specials).

Julia, who coordinates today's service, invites Saida to lead *adoración* – a time of slow choruses expressing repentance, commitment, and the desire for an intimate encounter with God.

Self-confident and in love with God and José Benito, Saida walks to the front, her curly hair smoothed into a barrette and her solid frame meticulously fitted in a self-tailored dress. She greets us with the invariable blessing, "*Dios les bendiga,*" and eloquently welcomes us to this opportunity to worship God. She steals a glance at song titles printed on the palm of her hand, then invites us to sing:

> *There is an anointing here, falling on me, filling me, satiating my being*
> *My heart and soul are being filled with the power of the Holy Spirit*
> *My life will never be the same.*

People sing passionately, with hands raised and eyes closed. They address a God who listens, kneel before a Jesus who gave his life for them, and welcome a powerful Holy Spirit who comforts and works miracles.

> *Renew me, Lord Jesus; I no longer want to be the same*
> *Renew me, Lord Jesus; put your heart in me*
> *Because everything about me needs to be changed, Lord*
> *I need more of you.*

Twenty minutes later, *adoración* subsides like the sun melting into the horizon. People gradually conclude their singing, returning from worship as if waking from dreams. They wipe their eyes, blow their nose, and rise from their knees or move back from the aisles to their seats.

Saida returns to her bench, and Julia invites Víctor to lead the time of *alabanza*. Víctor gives us a playful smile, invites us to stand, and asks, "Who lives?"

The children respond to their Sunday school teacher with enthusiasm, "Jesus!" Víctor frowns, his eyes dancing, and complains that we sound sleepy.

He asks again, "Who lives?"

We all shout together, "Jesus!" waking Anival's dog, Rambo, sleeping in the doorway.

Víctor compliments our improvement and leads us in a lively chorus:

> God's love is marvelous!
> God's love is wonderful!
> It's so high, I cannot rise above it.
> (We all stretch our arms high.)
> It's so deep, I cannot sink below it.
> (We bend down low.)
> It's so wide, I cannot go around it.
> (We open our arms wide.)
> God's love is so wonderful!
> (Most of us spin in a circle.)

We sing an uninterrupted series of similar, upbeat choruses. Anival shouts the lyrics at the top of his lungs, maintaining near perfect beat with a tambourine, while Goyo accompanies on the guitar, strumming like a mariachi with the four fingers on his right hand. (He lost his thumb when intervening in a tussle between his childhood dog and a cornered iguana.) We clap more or less in unison – until Víctor introduces a contemporary song he learned from the Christian radio station, and the unfamiliar music causes our admirable rhythm to degenerate into the sound of popping corn. Even then, our enthusiastic voices resonate throughout the village.

Many songs of *alabanza* reflect the concept of praise as warfare in which we fight the enemy and his evil influences. Uncomfortable with the focus and violent images associated with this interpretaion of praise, Tim and I used to refrain from singing certain songs. Several months ago, José Benito, standing next to us in a midweek service and intrigued by our stubbornness, whispered, "You know we sing about spiritual enemies and not people, don't you?" His comments initiated a series of lively conversations about reconciling Jesus' message of love and nonviolence with different interpretations of the Old Testament and spiritual warfare.

Our dialogue led us to new appreciation for one another's views. At the same time, however, I questioned if I should be

so concerned about analyzing the words of songs. I wondered if my critical thinking allowed room to worship with my brothers and sisters who, regardless of the words, offer their songs as love songs.

Today the congregation sings with gusto:

> *Great is the Lord;*
> *marvelous are his mighty works*
> *And in the strength of his hand*
> *there is power – power to defeat!*

José Benito glances at us and grins because he knows we sing "power to love" instead of "power to defeat."

Singing reigns again during *especiales*, a time in the service open to spontaneous participation from church members.

As always, Anival marches to the front and belts out his favorite song:

> *Although others worship gods made of*
> *metal, wood, and bronze*
> *I will praise the name of Jehovah.*
> *Because I am a priest called to minister*
> *in his presence*
> *I will praise Jehovah's holy, blessed name.*

Old Benilda offers the final *especial*, dedicating it to God in appreciation for her grandchildren's visit. Accompanying herself on the guitar, she clears her throat and begins to sing, but her wobbly voice catches on the second verse. Chuckling, she launches into a series of lighthearted apologies and a quick prayer, then starts over again. The congregation joins in to help her through the song.

After making sure no one else would like to sing an *especial*, Julia invites young Sandra to help with the offering. Coins clink in the basket as we sing:

> *The widow gave all she owned,*
> *and her offering greatly pleased God.*
> *The rich only gave leftovers,*
> *and their offering displeased him.*
> *If you give sincerely, dear brother,*
> *God will richly bless you.*
> *If you give generously, dear sister,*
> *God will richly bless you.*

Offerings collected, Julia introduces the person who will give the sermon. I still contemplate the lyrics of the offertory song. Their impact reminds me that words work powerfully in me. And well-contemplated lyrics can still be sung as love songs.

PREACHERS AND TEACHERS

Saida tells me that Goyo is a preacher and José Benito is a teacher, because Goyo exhorts and José Benito instructs. Preachers appeal to the heart and emotions, while teachers speak to the mind and intellect – both nurture the soul. She adds that Tim and I are good teachers but that we are not preachers.

Goyo is the best preacher around although he never attended school. He became a Christian when he was twenty years old and immediately longed to read the Bible. Goyo tells us that God answered his prayers with the miracle of literacy. Now he owns two books: a big, black Bible and an even bigger Bible dictionary.

Goyo preaches in a strong, clear voice that exudes self-assurance and love for God. Without notes or outlines, he weaves together biblical texts, illustrations fresh from the rural countryside, and frank exhortation with innate skill and candidness. I listen to his spontaneous and intuitive message as one appreciates a work of art. I do not always agree with what he says but admire the gifts of this man educated and instructed by the Holy Spirit with the most basic tools.

Younger, more humble, and less outspoken than Goyo, José Benito teaches with cautious council and guidance. He glances at carefully prepared notes and writes key words on the blackboard, often asking the congregation to correct his spelling and inviting them to comment or ask questions.

José Benito's latest sermons reflect a self-confidence he lacked when we first met him. Perhaps this is due to his recent engagement to Saida or because the congregation affirms his gifts and hopes he will accept being named pastor rather than coordinator of the leadership team. (Old Benilda has already declared that, regardless of his official title, she considers José Benito her pastor – because he visits her, counsels her, and chops her firewood.)

José Benito insists he needs more experience before becoming a pastor. He informs us, however, that if he assumes the responsibility someday, he will change little about the church's current administration. No congregation he leads will get away with making church the pastor's responsibility; everyone has to contribute and work together to allow the body of Christ ("not the body of José Benito," he jokes) to function well.

"And I will still sign you up to teach," he warns us, smiling.

Old Benilda has already declared that, regardless of his official title, she considers José Benito her pastor – because he visits her, counsels her, and chops her firewood.

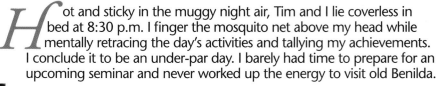

WORD AND DEED

*H*ot and sticky in the muggy night air, Tim and I lie coverless in bed at 8:30 p.m. I finger the mosquito net above my head while mentally retracing the day's activities and tallying my achievements. I conclude it to be an under-par day. I barely had time to prepare for an upcoming seminar and never worked up the energy to visit old Benilda.

Why do I so anxiously sift through daily events to settle on my accomplishments? Though I take seriously my responsibility to the North American churches that support me, I recognize my score-keeping as more than assuring myself that I earn my keep. My anxiety stems from something deeper.

Mennonite Central Committee workers are often inspired by Bible passages that emphasize the importance of demonstrating our faith through practical action. Several months ago, I shared a short devotional in church on James 2:14-17:

> *What is the use of saying you have faith if you don't prove it by your actions? That kind of faith can't save anyone. Suppose you see a brother or sister who needs food and clothing, and you say, "Well, goodbye and God bless you; stay warm and eat well" – but then you don't give that person any food or clothing. What good does that do? So you see, it isn't enough just to have faith. Faith that doesn't show itself by good deeds is no faith at all – it is dead and useless.*

After my devotional that day, I returned to my bench and continued reading in chapter three:

> *Not many of you should become teachers in the church, for we who teach will be judged by God with greater strictness.*

I read the passage as if standing in an austere celestial court of law, identifying the source of my frequent nighttime mathematics. Despite my claims to an intellectual equilibrium between faith and works, I fear judgement – perhaps my level of service fails to merit the privilege of teaching which I have assumed.

Tim and I work with a conference of twenty-one Costa Rican Mennonite churches to motivate congregations to serve their communities. A purpose for our presence is to emphasize the importance of demonstrating love for God by actively loving our neighbors. The very principles we teach encourage people to focus less on our words and more on how we live out our teaching.

Modeling a life of service is a big order to fill. This task would be less intimidating were it to imply serving others from only nine to five, but neither the Gospel nor our neighbors' needs respect work hours. For the most part, our neighbors demand very little of us, but their needs call out to me. Poverty, unemployment, illiteracy, alcoholism, and a host of other community needs weigh heavy on my conscience as we spend our days traveling, attending meetings, and coordinating workshops.

Never belittling or questioning our activities, our brothers and sisters provide immediate and practical expressions of God's love as a natural part of their daily routines. Economically poor yet rich in time, they freely offer their energy and limited resources to their neighbors. They chop Benilda's firewood, help Chepe build his house, give Nelda rice and beans, and assist Don Dimas in tending his field. Tim and I join in when our schedule allows, though I often feel we spend more time talking about service than actually serving.

In the sleeplessness of anxious moments, when I feel condemned by warnings such as Proverbs 25:14 (*A person who doesn't give a promised gift is like clouds and wind that don't bring rain),* I plead with God to conquer my fears. I am conscious of the incongruity between my self-criticism and his promise of peace.

My restless spirit almost inevitably hears God's voice; it commands my heart to be still. And if I am still, I hear God promise me that he loves me. He reminds me that service is simply gratitude, an echo of his love resounding in my life.

God also points me to my village brothers and sisters. When I find them in their rocking chairs, sitting on shady porches in hot, mid-day sun or watching the evening sunset, I pull up a chair and sit with them, soaking in their sense of identity that stands strong and alone, apart from anything they should or could be doing. Their peace defies the world's perception that they are poor, inferior, and insignificant, and gives honor to their Maker who has proclaimed them good.

Poverty, unemployment, illiteracy, alcoholism, and a host of other community needs weigh heavy on my conscience as we spend our days traveling, attending meetings, and coordinating workshops.

THE MISSIONARY

*B*alancing plates of rice, fried plantains, and beans, the congregation mills around the church after the meeting. Tim, José Benito, and I sit together on a sand pile, squeezing glasses of lemonade between our knees. Between mouthfuls, José Benito explains that he did not visit us yesterday because a neighbor needed help preparing his field for planting beans.

Our conversation pauses when Orlando walks up and extends me a kind hand. Orlando and his wife, Miseldi, live in the capital four hours away but are like family to the Cuatro Cruces congregation. They have served as missionaries and pastors in rural regions of the country and adopted over a dozen children from broken homes. Orlando is a long-time mentor to Cuatro Cruces leaders. However, since his appointment to the governing board of the Costa Rican Mennonite Conference, his visits have dwindled to only several a year.

Orlando shakes Tim's hand, then José Benito's, and explains his hasty departure by pointing to a bulky plastic bag full of clothes in the back of his old yellow Datsun, christened the *Misionero.* He finally came to take these clothes, which have been in his garage for months, to a family further up the road. We say we will see him when he drives back by on his way out of the village.

Backing the *Misionero* onto the road, Orlando pauses as a woman hails him and approaches the car. Seeing who she is, I stand up to leave. I brush the sand off my skirt and toss leftover rice to the chickens, eager to avoid hearing a familiar conversation.

We are accustomed to Josefa's appeals to people from out of town. When Josefa, her husband, and five small children arrived from Nicaragua a little over a year ago, the family played the congregation's heartstrings, asking for food and clothing until people's generosity wore thin. Church members became more reluctant to give the family their limited rations and instead invited Josefa and her husband to join them when they found paid work such as picking coffee, clearing fields, or digging wells. The couple only occasionally accepted the work opportunities and began approaching visitors from urban congregations. Their beautiful children often ended up with shiny, new notebooks, pencils, or toys, leaving the other kids wondering when God might come their way.

Josefa approached me for money until I asked too many questions and requested she express her needs to the church leadership. I told her that Tim and I would be glad to contribute to the congregation's response to her need. After that, Josefa stopped pulling us aside, though her children still frequent our home asking for money or food.

After the congregational lunch, Tim, José Benito, and I relax on our porch, enjoying the breezy afternoon. We sit in relative silence, listening to the rustling leaves and watching sun-dried clothes blow on the line like stiff cardboard cutouts.

Resting with our faces to the wind, we see Orlando returning from his visit to the family down the road. His car pulls over the hill, bumps toward us, and stops in the road in front of our house. Orlando beckons through the window, calling for José Benito.

From the porch, Tim and I listen to Orlando sharing with José Benito about Josefa's barefoot children. He reminds José Benito to obey Christ's call to reach out to people in need and find a way to get them shoes. He says he will try to bring some the next time he visits.

José Benito nods and remains silent. Orlando puts his hand on the young man's shoulder and assures him he is a good leader. Orlando knows José Benito well enough to forgive his noncommittal silence, unlike many others from the city who have experienced a similar reaction to their well-intentioned ideas on how to help Cuatro Cruces.

Orlando restarts the engine and the Datsun lurches toward the village entrance, rocking back and forth like a tiny boat traversing choppy waters.

José Benito returns to the porch, and we watch the old car melt into a dot and disappear over a hill – the *Misionero* from out of town.

Their beautiful children often ended up with shiny, new notebooks, pencils, or toys, leaving the other kids wondering when God might come their way.

CULTURE SHOCK

I silence the alarm boldly announcing 4 a.m. Falling back on the pillow, I open my eyes then shut them again, seeing only blackness either way. Reminding myself it is a travel day, I push down the sheet, untuck the mosquito net, and sit up to turn on the light. Tim climbs around me and heads out the back door to the bathroom. I set my feet on the cool cement floor and listen to him step into the shower, exhaling sharply under a chilly spray.

Showered and dressed, we grab clothes off the rack, examining them for scorpions before stuffing them into our packs. At 4:20 a.m., we turn out the lights and emerge from our nest onto a dark, muddy road. We whisper a word of thanks; stars twinkle in a clear sky and we have enough time to catch the bus.

José Benito is waiting for us at the bus stop – a cement block bench partially protected by rusty tin. (The roof is like a sieve when it rains and everyone under its shelter is forced to put up umbrellas.) Always rising before 5 a.m., José Benito greets us with an alert smile and cheery good morning. Ready for the quarterly church conference meeting in the capital, he carries a small duffel bag and his black shoes shine.

Don Dimas also waits at the bus stop. He wears a clean, button-down shirt that leaves his pronounced collarbones exposed. His belt is cinched to an extra hole punched in the leather, holding polyester pants to his wiry frame. He seems thinner than he used to be. Holding a worn duffel bag on his lap, he tells us that he finally has an appointment at the hospital after a six-month wait.

Hearing the bus approach, we gather our bags and side-step puddles between the bus stop and the road. We sigh as the bus slows; the seats are full and passengers already stand in the aisle.

Four hours later, Tim dozes in a seat several rows from me, finally off his feet after standing in the aisle for almost three hours. I stood for less than an hour before an old lady sitting near me tapped my arm and pointed to her seat – she was getting off soon. As her wrinkled hands urged me to sit down, I noticed a heavy-set woman eyeing me, then the empty seat. Trying to ignore her, I sank into the space by the window, feeling justified by the old lady's beckoning. Sleep eluded me, however, until the large woman found another seat thirty miles down the road.

I nudge Tim as we approach our bus stop near the airport. José Benito is still standing far down the aisle and Don Dimas rests in a seat near him. Tim rises and whistles to alert the two men of our approaching stop. We weave our way to the front, trying not to hit other passengers with our backpacks, then step off the stuffy bus into a different world.

Leaving behind sun-weathered faces and bodies toned by farm work, we are

> He seems thinner than he used to be. Holding a worn duffel bag on his lap, he tells us that he finally has an appointment at the hospital after a six-month wait.

Don Dimas

hemmed in by linen shirts, mini-skirts, beepers, briefcases, and Armani perfume. My face suddenly feels greasy and I suspect my deodorant has worn off. I remember that my jumper has bleach stains and realize I never washed our backpacks. Why did I forget to put on a bit of lipstick or mascara? I comb through knotty hair with my fingers then bend over to rub at red mud caked on my ankles, sandals, and between my toes.

Tim talks with José Benito and Don Dimas, who clutch their duffel bags to their chests as wide girths and full busts push past. Don Dimas' dark eyes squint anxiously at the signs on bus windows as vehicles speed by, honking and belching clouds of black fumes. An airplane roar catches him off guard and he watches the mechanical bird as it slices into a low-lying cloud. Tim taps his shoulder and points to a bus with a sign reading *Hospital San Juan de Dios*. Don Dimas nods, shakes our hands, and then timidly follows a tall man talking on a cell phone to the bus door. I hope he finds the right stop.

Tim, José Benito, and I take another bus to a neighborhood where we will attend the meeting. We arrive late and music already reverberates off the large sanctuary's ceramic floor and ornate ceiling. On stage, young, sharply dressed members of a band lead music for the pastors and leaders: a group of about forty-five men and ten women.

We find a seat near the back and join in the singing, trying to follow the unfamiliar lyrics of the latest contemporary songs, glad that amplified electric guitars, drums, and a keyboard drown out our hesitant voices.

I glance around as we sing, smiling and nodding to Genaro, from a village near Cuatro Cruces, Orlando, and many familiar faces from urban and rural congregations. Participants from rural churches have traveled up to seven hours to attend this one-day gathering. I wonder if they spent the night in the Conference headquarters and, if so, what they ate for dinner. When we stay with rural leaders in the noisy downtown office, we usually are the only two who dare venture into the city on our own. We bring fried chicken back to the office for everyone. Our rural friends rarely visit the city and express fear and great distaste for this urban jungle; according to television and relatives who have migrated here, it seethes with pollution, accidents, and crime.

After singing for a half-hour, the Conference evangelist (very much a preacher) invites us to take a seat and launches into a fiery sermon. The audience, charged with emotion, peppers his ardent words with *"Amen!"* and *"Alleluia!"*

Following the sermon, the Conference president continues the meeting with a PowerPoint presentation detailing his plan for church growth. José Benito, Genaro, and many other leaders and pastors listen respectfully despite foreign vocabulary and confusing diagrams; they never participate in discussion.

The president's plan perplexes me, and I question its relevance to churches in rural communities, where people constantly leave in search of work and congregations struggle to maintain a steady attendance. I also imagine that José Benito, Genaro, and many of the other *campesinos* are thinking about their fields: moist and waiting to be planted with beans.

Lunch and break times bring refreshing conversations with friends and pastors, many of whom sustain their families with a second job. We inquire about their congregations and plan visits for the coming months, appreciative of their hospitality and friendship.

The meeting concludes at 5 p.m., and Orlando invites Tim and me, José Benito, and Genaro to his home for the night. We accept, glad not to have to stay at the crowded Conference office. When we arrive at Orlando's cool, mountainside home, his wife, Miseldi, welcomes us and adds four more place settings to the large dining room table. While she finishes preparing dinner, we discuss the meeting with Orlando and three of their grown children. Silver-haired Orlando is the first Costa Rican Mennonite; he became a Christian in the 1960s through his friendship with a Mennonite missionary couple. He shares with the wisdom of

a person who has learned to ride the currents of numerous church trends.

At 4:30 the next morning, Orlando drives us in the *Misionero* to the bus stop downtown. At this hour, the city streets belong to taxis, hung-over drivers, and homeless people lining the sidewalks with their cardboard beds. I watch them through the window, wondering what it means for urban churches to reach out to people in need. I admire our friends who visit the homeless in the park, offering bread, coffee, and the Good News, and the congregation that goes out of its way to invite people from nearby slums. But these steps seem small and tentative and so many bodies line the streets. Perhaps that is why many urban congregations seem to ignore them, as I usually do when I walk downtown.

I notice José Benito also observing the street dwellers, and I wonder how people from Cuatro Cruces respond to this environment when they migrate to the city in search of work. What happens to their sense of community and ingrained custom of helping neighbors in need? I sigh, grateful yet feeling slightly guilty to be returning to a sleepy little village rather than staying in this colder, harsher world. We even have assigned seats for the bus trip home.

I notice José Benito also observing the street dwellers, and I wonder how people from Cuatro Cruces respond to this environment when they migrate to the city in search of work.

33

SHARING
THE JOURNEY

As Ellie and I wash dinner dishes, I reflect on the privilege of hosting her during her visits to Cuatro Cruces. The church eagerly anticipates her participation in services; her sermon this afternoon brought tears to people's eyes. Nelda told me afterwards that she has never heard a person teach with such grace.

I ask Ellie why she so enjoys coming to Cuatro Cruces from the city. She is one of the few from urban congregations who travel here without a car. She never complains about the long bus ride or the forty-five minute walk from the village entrance to our home. And I know the bus fare represents a financial burden with her modest salary as a health promoter.

Ellie's large, thickly-lashed eyes sparkle. Though her short stature is comparable to that of the Cuatro Cruces population, her fair complexion and delicate features distinguish her from the villagers. Her Spanish is soft and lilting. She answers my question with a smile. "The only thing difficult about escaping the city," she laughs, "is leaving my cat, Pearl, alone in my apartment." She continues, explaining her affinity to the poverty and down-to-earth faith of the people of Cuatro Cruces by telling a story.

Ellie's first encounter with God came in the form of a straightlaced little girl far

prettier and better fed than she. Anna's school uniform was always starched and ironed and her face rosy from a hot breakfast. She never arrived at school with the wild look Ellie recognized in her big sister after her mother beat her, and even saw in the mirror once. Nor did Anna's eyes ever dull like her own when her early morning cup of coffee finished splashing around in an empty stomach.

Though experience had taught her little more than "life's not fair" in her short seven years, Ellie's strong spirit resisted resignation and suspected the world of withholding more important lessons. Perhaps that is why she failed to hate Anna like her mother hated the woman she cooked and cleaned for every morning.

Anna was one of the pretty girls who always had the teacher smiling and boys pulling her braids. If she wanted, Anna could have participated in that carefree dance of life accessible only to beautiful people who never have to notice anyone plain or poor. But for some reason, Anna seemed attracted to Ellie.

It all started at recess the first day of first grade, when Ellie came in last in a scramble to reach the top of a tree in the school yard. Chest heaving and legs trembling, Ellie sat clutching the highest branches long after the rest of the children climbed down and ran to the rope swing. When she regained control of her legs, she slowly made her way down and plopped at the base of the nearby flagpole, scuffing her sister's old shoes as hot tears dripped onto the playground dust, making perfect circle grooves.

Head between her knees, Ellie took no notice of the little girl sitting next to her until her view of the moons in the dust was interrupted by half of a soft, white roll and a timid voice saying, "Here, take it. I'm not hungry anymore."

From that day on, sitting together and sharing Anna's snack became a daily ritual. As soon as the recess bell rang, Ellie would dash to the flagpole and sit staring at her sister's old shoes until Anna sat down beside her. Ellie never said anything as Anna unwrapped the soft, carefully prepared bundle – unleashing a delicious yeasty aroma of fresh-baked bread that summoned demons from her empty stomach. Out of the corner of her eye, Ellie would watch Anna break the roll and pass her an equal half. Then followed the shortest, sweetest minutes of Ellie's day.

One morning in April, after dozens of shared rolls, something snapped Ellie and Anna's ritual of broken bread. That sunny morning, Anna passed Ellie a piece that seemed like much less than half the roll, and the demons in Ellie's stomach clamored up into her throat. She heard herself shout, "Give me that, you spoiled baby!" as she yanked Anna's half of the roll from her young benefactor's startled grasp.

Bruising the bread with frightened fingers, Ellie sprang to her feet, ran across the playground, and hid behind an overflowing trash bin. She crouched like a fugitive animal, chest heaving, and stuffed her mouth full of forbidden morsels – waiting to yell back at God when he arrived to punish her.

At recess the next morning, Ellie returned to her hideout behind the trash bin and peered around the corner to watch for Anna. Anna soon appeared and sat at the flagpole as always, apparently unfazed by her snack companion's absence. She pulled the soft, cloth-wrapped bundle from her bag and untied the cloth's four corners. The fresh-baked smell mushroomed out like a genie escaping a bottle and accosted Ellie with full force, taunting, "Never again, never again!" Ellie tried to pull her eyes from Anna slowly chewing her roll, but they were captive. As she watched, the wildfires in her eyes slowly extinguished into dull, cold charcoal. Spent, she turned her head and leaned against the trash bin.

Then God ambushed her. Ellie heard footsteps approaching her hideout and opened her eyes just as Anna came around the corner of the bin. Pale, her lips pressed together, Anna dropped a soft, carefully wrapped bundle in Ellie's lap. "This is for you. My mom says I can bring you a roll every day," she whispered, then retreated as the recess bell announced a little girl's first taste of the Bread of Life.

> Out of the corner of her eye, Ellie would watch Anna break the roll and pass her an equal half. Then followed the shortest, sweetest minutes of Ellie's day.

WONDERING WHAT LIES AROUND THE BEND

After two weeks of traveling to visit churches in other regions, the last two hours of the trip home feel endless. The bus finally stops at the entrance to Cuatro Cruces and we yank our heavy packs from the overhead rack, weave through standing passengers clogging the aisle, and step down into a relentless, mid-day sun. The usual forty-five minute walk will take longer in this heat.

"Ah ha!" hollers Anival when he sees us coming up the road, our faces red and sweaty by the time we near his house. "Who are these strangers? We barely recognize you anymore!" he laughs, echoing the words we often hear his mother say with a smile as we return from trips.

Disheveled and dirty as usual, Anival gallops toward us on a broomstick. A twig that I assume he imagines a gun is tucked into his waistband. He flashes his characteristic, charming smile and extends a grimy hand. I clasp it, unusually big and callused for a nine-year-old, then ask him what in the world happened to his thumbnail. A black scab of dried blood and dirt clings to where his nail should be.

From the porch, Auxiliadora answers for her son: "Naughty boy! He sliced it trying to open a coconut with a machete. I told him to stay away from those trees."

"Knuckle-head," scoffs his seven-year-old cousin Delvin, whose mission in life seems to be pestering Anival.

I hold Anival's hand and ask him if he cried a lot when it happened. Anival shakes his head no. "He screamed bloody murder," Auxiliadora contradicts.

"He's a baby," adds Delvin.

Having mastered years ago the art of ignoring constant taunts and criticism, Anival pulls his hand from mine and runs off, this time positioning the broomstick as an unwieldy sword. Delvin takes off in pursuit.

Auxiliadora leans against the door. "School starts in a week," she sighs. "I'm thinking about putting him in again."

I remember this conversation from last year. Anival reenters first grade every school year wearing the same increasingly tight uniform and joining kids increasingly younger than he. His class inevitably includes boys with the same mission as his cousin Delvin, and he quickly falls out of favor with the teacher and students alike. Before long, either the teacher demands he leave or Anival refuses to attend. Auxiliadora yields and Anival drops out, undaunted by the greater task of entertaining himself for another long school year.

Anival is the youngest of Auxiliadora's six children. He was born after Auxiliadora's husband returned to Nicaragua, leaving her in Cuatro Cruces with five small children. Auxiliadora went to the capital to work in a factory and returned to the village a year later with money to buy a few cows – and a big belly. Anival has met his dad but never mentions him and could not tell you his name.

I often wish I could take Anival home, scrub through the layers of dirt until he is squeaky clean, cut his hair, and dress him in clothes just his size. I imagine taking him by the hand and walking with him to school, sitting in the desk next to him, and accompanying him through the day. Then if anyone were to pick on him they would have to pick on me too.

"Aunt Auxiliadora!" Delvin runs up to the porch and interrupts, "Anival's in the pasture with the calf again!" Delvin's impish smile reveals obvious delight in furnishing the incriminating news.

"Anival!" yells his half-brother, Víctor. "Get away from there! I told you to stay away from that calf!"

Anival has ventured into the family's pasture and is crouching next to a day-old calf that has been rejected by its mother. The calf trembles on his new legs and bleats feebly from hunger and fear. Anival looks up; he has the animal's umbilical cord wrapped around his hand.

"Let go of the cord, Anival!" Víctor yells. "If you pull it off, he'll bleed to death."

"He's already going to die," retorts Anival. "He's been abandoned!" He unwinds the cord from his hand, makes his way back across the field, and climbs through the fence.

I ask Víctor if it is true that the calf will die. Víctor says he might, if the other nursing cow refuses to adopt him or if he cannot adjust to drinking out of a bottle. Auxiliadora listens, squishing an ant into the wood wall with her finger. "It will be a struggle," she reckons, "but he will live."

Anival picks up the broomstick lying on the ground and mounts it, grinning as he trots past me on his fearless steed. Where will life take this boy, with his good-natured spirit and heart hardening to pain? He gallops down the road, valiant and never questioning his rough journey.

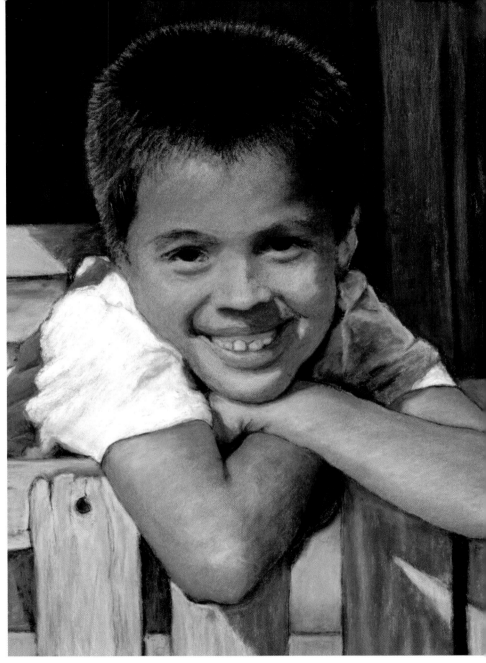

Anival

Nelda's girls at the Cruce

THE CRUCE

Nelda lives at one of several intersections in the Cuatro Cruces road. *Cuatro Cruces* can be translated as "Four Intersections" or "Four Crosses;" villagers prefer the former definition.

Nelda's wood home is small and dark, with a covered porch that looks out onto the intersection. Though plants potted in rusty paint cans brighten the exterior of the house, its interior is virtually empty, save for a bench, a table, and two rough-hewn beds.

Nelda's three daughters, two of them twins, seem to intuitively predict when I will walk through the *cruce*. They invariably stand at a big, open window that faces the intersection and wave to me. All three are shy like their mother, so they say nothing; they just smile beautifully and wave, their wisps of bodies like slender reeds in the wind.

I return their smiles – those merry smiles that reveal gentle spirits and tender buds of life. But my insides ache, lamenting their struggle to grow in the impoverished soil of family disintegration and suffering.

Nelda's husband left her just before Christmas and now lives a couple kilometers down the road with the teenage daughter of an important family in the church. He occasionally drops by his former home to leave a bag of rice or a week's supply of lard. He stopped by once when I was on the porch reading with the girls. He never looked at me or said a word.

Neighbors frequently give Nelda beans, rice, and yucca to supplement her daughters' diet, but the girls' slight frames never fill out with pre-adolescent plumpness. Many villagers are concerned. Auxiliadora sometimes lifts the oldest girl off her feet and gathers her in her big, soft arms. "Look," she exclaims, "she's so skinny I can almost hold her like a baby."

Nelda and the girls attend church on Sundays, and the twins often stop by our house on the way home from school. We color together, eat cookies, and drink lemonade. Then I tell them they need to go home before it begins to rain. I stand on the porch, powerless, and watch them run for the *cruce*.

RESURRECTION SUNDAY

Flushed and crying, a neighbor stumbles into church on Maundy Thursday, interrupting the midweek service. In tears, she pours out a jumble of words that stop my breathing though I do not quite capture their meaning. I hear the words "Goyo," "Don Dimas," and "motorcycle." The congregation suspends the service, lays hands on the woman, and prays for her and the family.

Once the service resumes, I lean over and whisper questions to Julia seated beside me. She explains that Don Dimas' son, daughter-in-law, and three-year-old grandson were on their way to swim in a nearby river when his son lost control of the motorcycle. The couple had not yet saved enough money to buy Ricardito a helmet.

We visit the grieving family at Don Dimas' house on Good Friday. Don Dimas is resting in bed, far weaker than he should be with what the doctor diagnosed as an ulcer. The house and yard are alive with activity: children playing, men conversing, women preparing coffee and food, and neighborhood dogs roving for scraps. The boy's body has been taken to the morgue in the capital for a mandatory autopsy, so the family postpones the customary all-night vigil, waiting for permission to retrieve the body. Everyone speculates about whether permission will be granted tomorrow or next week, since routine work grinds to a halt during Easter Week. Don Dimas' wife worries about being able to feed visitors for so long.

Dozens of community members come and go from the home and many stay around the clock. Neighbors bring food, prepare meals, and attend to other details of the vigil and funeral. Goyo, José Benito, Juan, and other local men clean the overgrown cemetery, select a plot, and dig a grave. Auxiliadora and Julia decorate the house and yard with brilliant bouquets of palm fronds, bougainvillea, hibiscus, and other blossoms. The flower arrangements match the artfully decorated crosses dotting the village roads for the Catholic *Vía de la Cruz* procession.

Ricardito's body arrives Easter evening, commencing the formal vigil. More than one hundred people remain all night long, conversing under a star-filled sky, singing choruses, viewing the little body, and simply being present. Tim and I stay until midnight, sitting on a big rock in the yard and watching the community care for its own.

Monday morning, under a low, fiery sun, the local teacher and school children arrive carrying small, bright bouquets. Dressed in their navy and white uniforms, the children form parallel, single-file lines with boys on one side and girls on the other. In perfect formation, they lead the funeral procession down the road to the cemetery. We sing choruses as we walk, accompanied by two guitarists: Goyo from the Mennonite church and Don Dimas' son from the Catholic.

The community buries the boy with sunshine, music, flowers, and tears. They offer a sorrowful, corporate prayer to the living God: a plea for consolation, a hope and claim for life beyond the grave.

My eyes well with tears; I deeply admire our neighbors as they reach out to comfort a suffering family. Tim and I struggle to help promote programs that will motivate church members to serve their communities, but have we ever witnessed such solidarity as we experience this Easter Week? How can we encourage the spirit of service present here? There is something graceful, natural, and bright about these days that a program alone will never inspire.

Funeral bouquet

DETERMINATION

Salvador has a limp and I am female, so neither of us participates in the church's first-ever soccer tournament. Instead, we watch from the sidelines with his beautiful six-year-old daughter, Sandra. Neither father nor daughter is one for many words, though both generously offer their merry laughter and kind smiles. Sandra, minus two front teeth, has her father's smile.

We sit near the Cuatro Cruces goal shouting encouragement whenever players come our way, but the ball rarely makes it this far down the field. The rest of the fans have gravitated to the action at the other end, so we observe in relative silence, enjoying the coolness of the cloudy day.

As we watch the soccer players exercise, I cannot help but think about Salvador's atrophied leg. I rarely stop to consider his handicap since he is strong and agile in spite of it. During our years in Cuatro Cruces, Tim and I have planted corn with him, felled trees, dug trenches, and watched him climb high into citrus trees to retrieve bright yellow oranges for us to take home. (Eyes full of laughter, he tossed oranges down to us, picking until our burlap sacks weighed far more than we could ever carry.) Only when walking with him do I notice his slow gait, hampered by a dragging leg, and appreciate his extra efforts to sustain a *campesino's* rigorous routine.

Curious about Salvador's history, I ask him how old he was when he contracted polio. Salvador smiles, his arm draped around his daughter, then takes me back to his childhood thirty years earlier. For a few moments, Sandra and I walk with him in his native Nicaraguan village, enjoying the story and the gentle cadence of his voice.

By the time he was five years old, Salvador already helped his father and older brothers cultivate corn, sorghum, and red beans. He remembers working in the fields and vividly recalls his parents' suffering when polio swept through town, settling in the bodies of five children. Salvador was one of the two who survived the illness and the only one who ever walked again.

Two agonizing months after contracting the illness, when Salvador improved enough to sit up in bed, his grandfather carved two rough crutches and urged him to stretch his withered legs. His numerous falls soon diminished, his raw underarms callused, and Salvador learned to walk with his three legs almost as well as most boys do with two – but it just was not the same. After a frustrating attempt to plant beans in rainy-season mud with crutches, the strong-willed boy decided a man must walk on his own two legs.

Salvador's attempts to shed his crutches made his mother protest that she could not take any more of her little boy's suffering. His father, giving in to his wife's tears, bought Salvador a horse. "A man can do almost anything on a good animal," he explained to his son. Soon the village never saw Salvador without his horse.

"But a man can't be a farmer on a horse," Salvador tells me, shaking his head. His father's efforts to keep him busy hauling seed and taking water to his brothers in the fields never satiated his desire to plant and swing a machete.

"Determination," Salvador looks at me, "allowed me to walk again, brought me a hundred miles across a mined border into Costa Rica, and puts food on the table every day for my wife and little girl. Determination can get you most anywhere," he tells me, grinning. "It can even get a woman into a soccer game."

Little Sandra laughs aloud, her coffee-colored face breaking into a radiant smile. When she grows up, she declares, no one will stop her goals.

Salvador was one of the two who survived the illness and the only one who ever walked again.

Planting season

UNLESS A SEED

Don Dimas is withered and gray like a dry, spindly branch. He has almost succumbed to cancer. His chest heaves as we pray with him. Next to me, Doña Aide sobs quietly and clenches my arm. I grope for words that will embrace them longer than our presence and surround them with love. Finding none, I say nothing. We sit in silence, crying, as Don Dimas leans on the bedroom windowsill, hiding his face.

Doña Aide whispers that the rainy season will arrive soon, but their fields are destined to remain empty and sterile. Tim assures her that he will help plant their corn as soon as the rains soften the sun-baked ground. "I have become a good farmer," Tim says, reminding her of our first planting lessons, "because the best farmer in town was my teacher." Don Dimas smiles weakly, groaning with the pain of waning life. Tears roll down Tim's cheeks as he witnesses his friend's agony, and he assures Don Dimas that the two of them will plant together again – if not here, then in heaven, where the harvest is always plentiful.

Two weeks later, after a long, gentle rain, Tim starts to clear Don Dimas' land for planting. Hearing of his intentions, eight men from church join him in the fields. Several of them are new to the church and recently reconciled with God, their wives, and their children. The men banter and sing as they work, laughing about keeping their distance from the *gringo's* machete.

After three days of clearing and planting, they decide they so enjoyed working together that they will plant their fields collectively this season, just like the good old days. And they make the pact there in the field, confirming a first fruit of Don Dimas' land.

WHOLENESS

"How are Saida and José Benito? And what about Víctor?" I pause from sorting papers to read the old postcard from a member of last summer's work-and-learn team. Seven members of a Canadian church spent two weeks working alongside and learning from the Cuatro Cruces congregation. The group's letters never failed to mention these three village youth.

During the Canadians' visit, Víctor and Saida unabashedly entertained the group with nonstop chatter in Spanish, peppered by newly acquired English phrases. Their sparks of mischief constantly lit wildfires of laughter as newfound friends sawed and pounded and painted together on the new classrooms.

Young Víctor adopted Margaret, the eldest visitor, and taught her how to hold a hammer and nail, sit on a board while he sawed, and say "tired" in Spanish. By the end of the week, Margaret declared that she believed in Víctor's talent and would sponsor his university studies. We announced the good news to Víctor, emphasizing his responsibility in taking initiative in applying to schools.

Saida paired up with Amy, the youngest and most inquisitive Canadian, and the two of them became pros in Spanglish. By the end of the week, bubbly Saida understood dozens of English phrases, and Amy had so improved her second language she looked forward to skipping a level of high-school Spanish. They promised they would write in each other's languages.

Doug and Juan's friendship flowered on the Canadians' last day in Cuatro Cruces. After the Costa Rican and Canadian group finished building the classrooms, Víctor invited the group on a two-hour hike to a waterfall. Doug, recently diagnosed with a debilitating illness, was unprepared for the challenging trek. Slowly making his way along the steep, slippery trail, he allowed the other hikers to go ahead of him, but Juan refused to leave his side. Doug survived the hike by depending entirely on Juan's strong shoulder and a walking stick the young man had carved for him. Sheer determination, bolstered by Juan's patient encouragement, enabled him to persevere.

Back in Cuatro Cruces after the hike, Doug flopped in our hammock and admitted he would have never dared the hike had he known what

Their sparks of mischief constantly lit wildfires of laughter as newfound friends sawed and pounded and painted together on the new classrooms.

lay ahead. But, he explained, he also would have missed what had been one of the most meaningful experiences of his life – depending on the help of his Costa Rican brother.

A month later, Juan received the first letter ever sent to him. He grinned ear-to-ear as he read Doug's words of appreciation for saving him on the jungle hike. But he never wrote back. Doug probably knows Juan never writes.

Saida and Amy corresponded for a while, until this present life slowly blurred the memories that first enlivened fresh, photographed faces.

Margaret wrote frequently to inquire about Víctor's progress in applying for school. Víctor never took the initiative to look into study opportunities, I had to reply, and if he hesitates to light the fire he will never be able to keep it burning. Margaret's communication endured even after the disappointing news. Her unusual perseverance and hand-made cards to Víctor and other friends, though rarely answered, won their great affection.

Facilitating a work-and-learn team provided me with a new perspective on my own short-term cross-cultural experiences. I remember eagerly promising myself I would hang on to those relationships, that I would faithfully write and visit again sometime. I occasionally fulfilled my promises by saying a prayer for my Venezuelan host family or writing Ecuadorian work partners. Tim and I even visited Honduran friends.

I recall hundreds of faces as I leaf through my mental scrapbook. Silence is disrespectful, forgetting sacrilege – but so often I struggle to remember their names.

I sit with my elbows on the table and my head in my hands. What will happen to the faces and names of my brothers and sisters here? I can hear the women laughing next door during their Tuesday fast. Could the vividness of these days ever fade?

My father tells me, during big moves or transitions, when my heartstrings get hooked as I say goodbye, that life is a series of farewells. If you refuse to accept any time as a goodbye time, he says, you spend your life looking over your shoulder, feeling like a book has been taken from you only half read. Instead, he tells me, delight in the wholeness of your memories and accept their lessons. Then open a new cover and discover fresh voices. Someday, in crisp pages, you might recognize them from something you have already read.

Benilda

ON GOODBYE

*T*hese are days of heightened senses. I break down each moment into tiny fragments and touch them, smell them, probe them, wondering when they will escape me.

I love these days with an idealized love. These indigo mountains are too beautiful, and even the stones in the road sparkle like gems. I try to shake departure's romance with reminders of clouds, sweat, and tears; it makes memories too rich, too heavy on my heart.

The familiar rhythm, voices, songs, and prayers usher me through our last church service with our Cuatro Cruces friends. We raise our hands, eyes closed, offering grateful prayers and songs of *alabanza* and *adoración*. Feeling travel companions by my side, I sing love songs.

During *especiales*, Anival marches to the front of the church to sing his favorite song: *"Although others worship gods made of metal, wood and bronze…"*

Benilda announces a song as thanks to God for our time in Cuatro Cruces. Accompanying herself on the guitar, she clears her throat and begins to sing.

The room is quiet and tears stream down our faces as we listen, grieving the end of this walk together.

José Benito invites the congregation to ask God to protect and guide us. The sanctuary fills with a sound like ocean waves as our brothers and sisters pray for our journey. I know from earlier conversations that our friends imagine us continuing along roads like these – yet even better, they promise, because we will walk together with grandparents, parents, siblings, and other relatives. They always wondered how we could be so far away from our families.

After the service, Julia, Auxiliadora, and Benilda rush to fill bowls and glasses for the congregational meal – a farewell gift to us – and the children line up for the feast. Benilda serves me and Tim first, with saffron-colored rice mounded high in our bowls.

Our last hours together resemble hundreds before them, as if we uphold an unspoken agreement to avoid awkward ceremonies or speeches. I am grateful, since words would be poor vehicles for my feelings. Adults leisurely eat and converse while children hurry to finish their meals so they can play in the yard. An hour later, the meal over and kitchen cleaned, friends approach us to say goodbye. My eyes are dry and emotions numb as I hug them as if I will see them again tomorrow.

In the afternoon, eager to escape the stillness after so many farewells, Tim and I invite young Sandra and Anival to a game of soccer. We play around one of the goalposts, four mere dots on the vast soccer field. Sandra kicks the ball through my legs and Anival celebrates the goal with a cartwheel. The distant volcanoes solemnly observe the tussle and laughter of children.

Our knees caked with red mud from the soccer field, we ride our bikes to Doña Aide's house. We find her in the kitchen preparing tortillas ground from the corn Tim planted with the men from church. She watches me attempt to shape a tortilla, and I delight in the laughter returning to her grieving eyes. We savor the hot tortillas with fresh cheese; they taste like those early days in the fields.

Evening light pours in Julia's doorway when we stop by on our way home. Her kitchen table proudly displays guavas and eggs from Benilda, and she serves us coffee that Ana gave her. We drink the coffee with cookies I baked as a goodbye gift, wishing she could read the words printed on our mugs. I will remember her with a halo of sunlight on her hair.

José Benito and Saida wait for us in the hammocks on our porch. They bring fish as a farewell gift. We open the door and weave through boxes cluttering the house. (Orlando offered to take our luggage to the capital in the *Misionero*, freeing us to travel one last time by bus.) Saida fries the fish to a golden brown while we admire our memories – stories of two couples in love, full of friendship and romance.

These are days of heightened senses. I break down each moment into tiny fragments and embrace them.

THE ROAD DIVIDES

I silence the alarm boldly announcing 4 a.m. and fall back on the pillow. Reminding myself it is a travel day, I push down the sheet, untuck the mosquito net, and sit up to turn on the light. Tim climbs around me and heads to the bathroom. I set my feet on the cool cement floor, listening to him step into the shower and exhale sharply under a chilly spray. The end of the ritual feels so much like the ritual itself.

We walk in the moonlight toward the village entrance, shouting, *"Adios!"* as we pass our neighbors' houses. Most of them respond from their dark houses with a sleepy, *"Adios!"* Julia's windows glow with candlelight, and she comes to the door to assure us that she will be praying.

I travel this way for the last time, imagining Jesus walking alongside us. I watch him tread the uneven road, the stones bending his sandals, slowing his gait, and guiding his path. As we pass the moonlit houses, I imagine him greeting our friends, embracing each one. He reminds us we will live together again someday.

Light illuminates the cracks in the walls of Auxiliadora's house; the family waits for us with coffee and tears. Anival, his sister, and his grandpa insist on joining us for the remaining half-hour walk to the entrance. Old Don Gregorio, unhindered by my heavy backpack slung across his shoulder like a sack of beans, urges us to hurry, concerned that we might miss the bus.

I feel a knot in my throat as we approach the bus stop where the Cuatro Cruces road and the paved road meet. Birds and howler monkeys boisterously celebrate the new morning as gray dawn dissolves into sunshine.

Then it is over. I hug Anival and his sister and take my backpack from Don Gregorio as the bus appears around the bend and slows to a stop. Tim and I clasp the old man's callused hand and thank him for his help, then turn to climb the bus stairs. As the door closes and engine rumbles, we catch a glimpse of our three friends waving, then turning back toward Cuatro Cruces.

My emotions foggy with exhaustion, I lean my head against the seat. Something feels wrong about simply closing time's door on our experiences. I remember C.S. Lewis' description of heaven in *The Last Battle*: all that is good lives eternally, while suffering and sadness die out with our notion of time.

Yes, the past three years are a creation, formed out of the stuff of this world into something good and complete.

Somehow, the stones of this road, lasting far longer than even fading memories, will determine the way I go.

Leaving Cuatro Cruces

*L*eslie Hawthorne Klingler and her husband, Tim, work with the Mennonite Central Committee and are members of Lombard Mennonite Church in Illinois. They drink their coffee *con leche* and wear out their running shoes every ten months. They plan to attend seminary.

*D*otty Hawthorne is an artist living and painting in San Luis Obispo, California. Her watercolor and pastel paintings have won numerous awards and have been displayed in many group and solo exhibitions. She is represented by Aquarius Gallery in Cambria, California.